PowerHiking

LONDON

ELEVEN GREAT WALKS THROUGH THE STREETS OF LONDON AND ENVIRONS

CAROLYN HANSEN   CATHLEEN PECK

Art direction and design	Dennis Gallagher and John Sullivan
	Visual Strategies, San Francisco
Maps	Kina Sullivan
Photography	Carolyn Hansen
Copy Editor	Elissa Rabellino
Cover photo	Svein-Magne Tunli
Additional photos	photo stock
Printer	NORCAL Printing, San Francisco
Publisher	PowerHiking Ltd.

PowerHiking

FOREWORD

The delightful English accent, roast beef, Yorkshire pudding, the Monarchy, pubs, high tea, Shakespeare, the Empire, the traditional ceremonies, the castles, the monuments, and the beautiful English parks draw us to visit England. We are all anglophiles at heart and needed no prodding to *PowerHike* London. We worked on our advance planning with great anticipation and excitement, even though we have explored London many times over the years. Once again, by *PowerHiking* London we saw the city with fresh eyes, from one side of the River Thames to the other, and delved into the amazing history, the cultural influences of the monarchy, the incredible architecture housing the seats of government, and the ubiquitous construction projects bringing London into the new millennium and to the forefront of contemporary architecture. The River Thames, once home to pirates, now ferries commuters to beautiful waterfront condominiums with amazing views back to the city. New laws limit cars within the city. The whole country is waking up to environmental responsibility, as evidenced by this year's theme for the Chelsea Garden Show— GREEN! We saw an ever-changing London, alongside the familiar and beloved historical London. It was beautiful, exciting, and most of all—fun!

We measured our time and distances with a GPS device and diligently noted the names of shops and pubs. The restaurants, pubs, and stores we mention have been in business for years, some for centuries. While they may change somewhat, we hope that you find them as fascinating as we did. There will be slight variations as you do the hikes and in your destinations. Everyone walks at a different pace and will spend more or less time exploring points of interest. The museums and castles are destinations where you can spend much more or much less time, depending on your own agenda. Any mistakes in the directions or the maps are ours, and we hope that you will forgive small inaccuracies.

We are continually grateful to our power partners, John and Rodney, for their support of our endeavors. Our design team, John Sullivan and Dennis Gallagher, continue to amaze us with their talent and creativity.

Carolyn Hansen, Cathleen Peck

THINGS TO KNOW, BEFORE YOU GO

YOUR STYLE IN LONDON

London can be damp and there is frequently a light foggy drizzle. It rains often and cool weather is the norm. There is the occasional warm spell, but most of the year it is cool. Londoners generally dress with conservative, fashionable style, and appropriately for the weather. Bring comfortable clothes such as jackets and slacks, pantsuits, and stylish, comfortable walking shoes. You will see jeans but usually only on tourists. Layering is the key. Be prepared with sweaters to layer under coats and jackets. A light raincoat and a small, packable umbrella are recommended. Since your shoes may get wet, bring a second pair of comfortable walking shoes or a pair that is water-resistant. You will be comfortable in any weather, and ensure that you are welcomed into traditional London.

GETTING ABOUT THE CITY

The taxi system in London is quite good. While not cheap, it is very reliable. The taxi drivers study for two years and must pass extensive exams before being issued a taxi license. They are very knowledgeable on the city and its history and are terrific tour guides. The tube (underground) is an easy, inexpensive way to get about the city. It is well marked, easy to follow, and clean. There are riverboats plying the River Thames and you can disembark and re-embark in most tourist locations. The train system is also quite easy to use, very accessible, and relatively inexpensive.

SECURITY

As in all large cities, there are elements looking for an easy mark. Be especially vigilant in crowds and on public transportation. Do not exhibit large amounts of cash, flashy jewelry, or call attention to yourself as a visitor. Sometimes, people working in pairs will try to distract you while grabbing your wallet, purse, and camera or cell phone. Keep these secure on your person, and be aware of your surroundings. There are now thousands of security cameras on the streets of London. These will probably photograph you many times. It is meant as a deterrent, not to invade privacy.

RESTAURANTS AND PUBS

While restaurants in London can be quite expensive, pubs and cafes are much more reasonable, lots of fun, and serve good food. Some typical English pub food includes steak and kidney pie, Shepherds' pie, and fish and chips. (Chips are French fries and potato chips are called "crisps") If you dine at a popular restaurant, it is necessary to have advance reservations. You can email or fax reservations from home ahead of time. You can also ask the concierge at your hotel to arrange a table for you. The diversity of the city is reflected in the food and there are wonderful restaurants for every type of cuisine. The value of the pound versus the dollar can be quite a shock to Americans who discover that breakfast in the hotel can be very costly! Look for a hotel that includes breakfast in the room charge. Tip: Look around the neighborhood for a self-serve café where Londoners go for a light meal. The food is usually fresh and good. Some good suggestions are Pret A Manger and Café Nero. Most restaurants include the gratuity in the check, but ask if it is not clearly stated.

CREDIT CARDS

Before you go, alert your credit card companies that you plan to travel to England. This will prevent a possible denial of charges because of suspicion of a stolen card.

COURTESY

The English are unfailingly courteous, whether you meet a taxi driver, a shopkeeper, or the hotel doorman. They go out of their way to be helpful to tourists. Show your respect for them by courteous interaction and a pleasant attitude.

OBTAINING CASH

There are ATMS everywhere in London, so no need to bring more than 100 pounds with you for the taxi ride to your hotel, gratuity for the bellman, and the like to get started.

WEB SITES

The royal family has posted a new web site, www.royal.gov.uk. Visit it before your trip for interesting historical information, events, ceremonies, and updates on tour times.

WHAT IS POWERHIKING?

PowerHiking is walking with an agenda that excites not only your senses but also your spirit. It takes walking to a new level of energy and interest and allows you to see and to do as much as possible. Your days are full of exhilarating experiences and exercise. *PowerHiking* lets us see more of the unexpected—an amazing view, an ancient passageway, charming lampposts, and royal crests. In London, *PowerHiking* takes on a whole new meaning. The city is bursting with power: royal, military, cultural, and economic. London is a city full of history while at the same time a city of change. Skyscrapers rise next to venerable historical icons in the cityscape; commuter ferries dot the infamous River Thames, reminiscent of schooners of bygone days. The power of diversity in the city is striking as well. Londoners come from all over the world, speaking English with the clipped accent that is a product of the British Empire.

Although we spend very full days *PowerHiking* the richness that is London, the walks can be divided into less strenuous excursions, with more time devoted to the pleasures of pubs, high tea, art museums, historical monuments, parks, and gardens. You may choose to spend only a few hours exploring the city or follow the longer routes that take you through the many historical sites. The city is truly a feast to enjoy, as you prefer. You are in charge of your experience, and walking from one destination to the next is the key! Wear your *PowerHiking* shoes, take a bottle of water, a camera and this book, and head out on your London *PowerHike*!

CONTENTS

CHAPTER ONE

THE ROYAL WALK

WELLINGTON ARCH

GREEN PARK

BUCKINGHAM PALACE

ST. JAMES'S PARK

WHITEHALL

WINSTON CHURCHILL WAR MUSEUM

WESTMINSTER CATHEDRAL

BIG BEN

PARLIAMENT

QUEEN'S MUSEUM

ROYAL MEWS

TIME All day   **DISTANCE** 13 plus miles
(possibly more if all tours are taken)

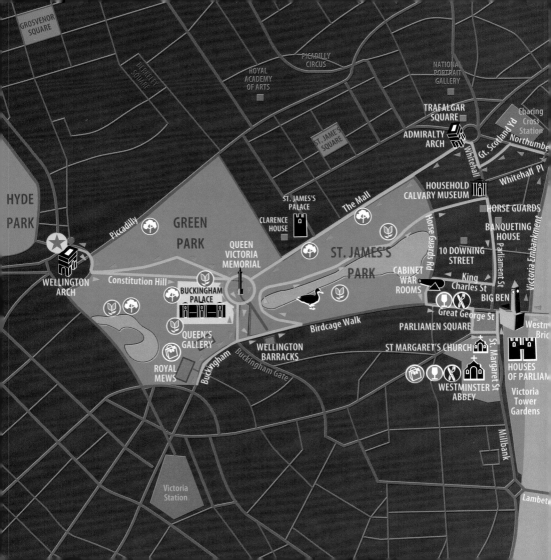

History, tradition, pomp, circumstance, military power, and the monarchy are at the heart of the British Empire and the London that we visit today.

This *PowerHike* is an adventure through English history as we explore seats of power, history, art, and tradition, and thrill at the richly produced ceremonies beloved by the English and watched for hundreds of years. We start this *PowerHike* at the Wellington Arch, across from Hyde Park, a landmark in London. Built in the early 1800s and designed by Decimus Burton, it is topped by the largest bronze sculpture in Europe. It is open to visit inside, and the views of the surrounding

parks are breathtaking. Before our

step into history, take a moment to

walk around the circle to observe the

monuments — tributes to soldiers in

the British Empire. There is the statue

of Wellington himself, as well as moving

monuments to soldiers who served from

New Zealand and Australia, soldiers

who served in the

Middle East, and soldiers who served in

World War I. Pass through the Arch and

walk up Constitution Hill. Green Park is

on the left, and the extensive gardens of Buckingham Palace are on the right. If

you have timed your walk in the morning just right, you can watch the Queen's

Horse Guard pass through the Wellington Arch on the way to Whitehall and

the changing of the Horse Guard. We will visit Whitehall shortly but first we

visit Buckingham Palace and the Changing of the Guard.

At Queen Victoria Memorial turn right, and you are in

front of Buckingham Palace in all its magnificence. The

Palace is the official London residence of the Monarch,

and is the location of ceremonies, receptions, and official

royal events. Find a spot among the crowd to watch the most famous and popular ceremony in London. The Changing of the Guard occurs daily at 11:30

a.m., May through July, and on alternating days during the other months when the Queen is in residence. You know when the Queen is residing at Buckingham Palace because the royal standard is flying above the Palace. As the Queen's Guard and band approaches from Wellington Barracks, you are immersed in this proud English tradition. There are five different regiments

of guards, distinguished by different uniform

badges but all wearing the famous red coat

and great helmet. There are fascinating tours

of the splendors of the State Rooms of

Buckingham Palace in summer while the Queen is in Scotland.

As Buckingham Palace is a working

royal residence, the State Rooms tour

is subject to change and security is

extensive. Admission is timed, and

advance tickets are recommended.

Enjoy the unique Changing of the Guard ceremony, and

then circle Queen Victoria Memorial to Birdcage Walk

to watch the Queen's

Guard and band

return to Wellington

Barracks. Wander

into St. James's Park, London's oldest park

and one of its prettiest. Colorful birds and

waterfowl abound, identified by markers along

the picturesque lake. St. James's Park is filled

with flowers and Londoners enjoying the

beauty. Exit St. James's Park at the Guard

Memorial and cross Horse Guard Road to

Horse Guards at Whitehall to watch the

changing of the Horse Guard. A new museum is open there as well. On the other side of the building is Whitehall. Turn right on

this very busy street and pass by Banqueting House (part of Whitehall Palace, a former royal residence) and the Ministry of Defense on the left, and Downing

Street on the right. You can glimpse 10 Downing Street, home of the Prime Minister, beyond the guards. At King Charles Street, turn right to the Churchill Museum and Cabinet War

Rooms. This mesmerizing historical site is definitely worth a visit. The bunker

was the headquarters of Winston Churchill during World

War II, where he and his cabinet conducted British wartime activity. It has been

maintained as it was when Churchill walked the corridors. The tunnel connects

Whitehall with Parliament, but Churchill lived down

in the war rooms throughout most of the war. The

new Churchill Museum provides captivating insight

into this courageous leader, his spirit, and the achievements for which he is

revered today. The Switch Room Cafe is available for refreshment and is a good

spot to contemplate what it was like to live in this environment. The shop will fascinate military history buffs.

Upon emerging from the museum, turn left on Horse Guard Road to Great George Street. Go left again to Parliament Square and cross to Westminster Abbey. This glorious cathedral is the place of last rest of kings, queens, and famous cultural figures. The wedding of Prince Charles and Princess Diana, as well as the funeral service for Princess Diana, were held here. It houses the Tomb of the Unknown Soldier and the Battle of Britain stained glass window, and has been the site for the coronation of each of Great Britain's monarchs.

The actual coronation chair, 800 years old and unused since the 1952 coronation of Elizabeth II, is on display. The architectural grandeur of this 13th century cathedral is awe-inspiring, so

allow enough time to appreciate its beauty.

Following your visit to Westminster Abbey, step into the priory and the bookstore. Exit and turn right to St. Margaret's Church. Originally built as a church for local parish inhabitants, it is known as the church of the House of Commons. Cross to Parliament Square to see the many bronze statues, most

notably the statue of Winston Churchill. In front

of you across Parliament Street are Westminster

Hall, the Houses of Parliament, and Big Ben, the

world's most famous clock tower. Bordered by

Victoria Tower Gardens and the River Thames,

these are undoubtedly the most iconic and photographed structures in Great

Britain. Parliament, with both the House of Commons and the House of Lords,

dominates the skyline from its splendid location on the river. Follow Bridge

Street to Westminster  Bridge and wander

across for glorious views back. Retrace your

steps back over the bridge to Victoria

Embankment, walking right along the river

to Northumberland Avenue. Turn left in the direction of Admiralty Arch. Pass under the arch and you will be on The Mall, frequently

decorated with the British Union Jack. Walk this tree-lined

avenue of ceremonial history traveled by kings and queens for

centuries. St. James's Park is on the left, St. James's Castle and

Clarence House (former home of the Queen Mother and current residence of

Prince Charles) on the right, and Buckingham Palace is in front of you. Clarence

House is open to guided tours in August and September, and much of the Queen

Mother's extensive art collection is on display. Tickets are timed and subject to change as Clarence House is a working royal residence. Veer left around Queen Victoria Memorial circle to Buckingham Palace Road and the Queen's Gallery which houses a rotating collection of art, china, antiques, furniture, and other treasures from the royal collection. It is open daily. Just beyond the Queen's Gallery on Buckingham Palace Road is The Royal Mews. Not only are the magnificent royal horses trained in this working stable, but also you will see the royal carriages and the glorious gold state carriage used only for coronations. The Cleveland Bays are a British breed of carriage horse and the Windsor Grey always pull the Queen's carriage. This is an

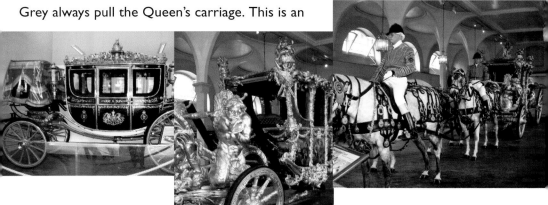

enthralling and very worth while tour, and The Royal Mews is open May through

October. If you did not visit the extensive gift shops on the tour of the State

Rooms or the Queen's Gallery, do visit the gift shop at The Royal Mews. All

three shops have unusual books, toys, and royal replicas for purchase. Retrace

your steps on Buckingham Palace Road, veering left in front of Buckingham

Palace at Queen Victoria Memorial circle and through the magnificent gates

into Green Park. Frequented by Londoners enjoying the out-of-doors, the park

has sun chairs for  rent (as they are in all

of London's parks). Green Park was designed

so that monarchs could travel from palace to palace without leaving royal grounds. Wander through the park, being sure to see the Canadian Monument,

and head in the direction of the Wellington Arch and the end of this history-laced *PowerHike.* We have ventured through England's glory, its seats of power, royalty, traditions, and ceremonies. You have passed many pubs and restaurants.

Now is a good time to visit one to soak up a little more English atmosphere while taking time to reflect on all that you have experienced today.

Note: It is possible to purchase one ticket, known as the Royal Day Out, which admits you to the State Rooms, the Queen's Gallery, and The Royal Mews at a discounted cost.

TIME   All Day   **DISTANCE**   **10** plus miles

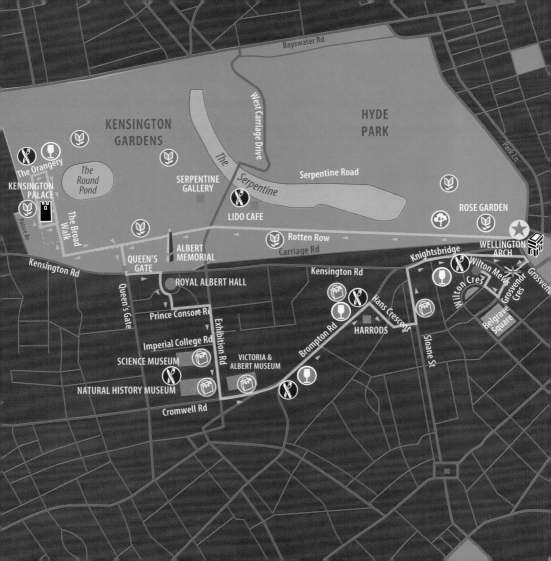

Bayswater Rd

KENSINGTON
GARDENS

West Carriage Drive

HYDE
PARK

Park Ln

The Orangery

KENSINGTON
PALACE

The
Round
Pond

SERPENTINE
GALLERY

The Serpentine

Serpentine Road

ROSE GARDEN

LIDO CAFE

Palace Av

The Broad Walk

QUEEN'S
GATE

ALBERT
MEMORIAL

Rotten Row

Carriage Rd

WELLINGTON
ARCH

Kensington Rd

Knightsbridge

Wilton Mews

Kensington Rd

ROYAL ALBERT HALL

Kensington Rd

Wilton Cres

Grosvenor

Queen's Gate

Prince Consort Rd

Hans Crescent

Belgrave
Square

Grosvenor Cres

Imperial College Rd

Exhibition Rd

HARRODS

Sloane St

SCIENCE MUSEUM

VICTORIA &
ALBERT MUSEUM

Brompton Rd

NATURAL HISTORY MUSEUM

Cromwell Rd

This *PowerHike* takes you to Hyde Park, a beautiful oasis of green in the middle of London. We begin at Hyde

Park Corner, across from the Wellington Arch and the Wellington Museum. The museum, former home of the Duke of Wellington, is open daily and worth a visit and step back into history. As you pass through the magnificent Hyde Park gates, turn left onto Rotten Row. A wide path that parallels Kensington Road,

Rotten Row got its catchy name from the old "Route de Roi" or King's Road. Dating from the

17th century

during the reign of William III, it was originally used as a shortcut between Buckingham Palace and the royal country home, Kensington Palace. On your left is a bridal path, and if you are *PowerHiking* between 9 and 10 in the

morning, you will Horse Guard riding across from Hyde Road to the changing

see the Queen's from their barracks Park on Kensington of the Horse Guard at Whitehall. You will encounter runners, walkers, bicyclists, and others enjoying this beautiful park. The Rose Garden and

Holocaust Memorial Garden are on the right. Take a detour and amble through them, marveling at the beauty that surrounds you. Follow Serpentine Road along The Serpentine, a beautiful lake in the middle of Hyde Park. On warm days you will see people enjoying the day on the lawn on rented deck chairs.

The Serpentine has a boat house on the far side of the lake, where you can rent small row and paddle boats. Even in London's familiar gray weather, you will find many people enjoying the lake.

At the café, return to Rotten Row and continue in the direction of the Prince Albert Memorial. Cross West Carriage

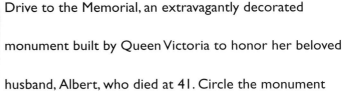

Drive to the Memorial, an extravagantly decorated monument built by Queen Victoria to honor her beloved husband, Albert, who died at 41. Circle the monument and continue left on Flower Walk

through the increasingly beautiful Kensington Gardens. At Broad Walk turn right in the direction of Kensington Palace. You will pass the Round Pond. On the left is a statue of Queen Victoria, and beyond, the entrance to the Palace.

Originally a country home, Nottingham House, it was converted into a palace by Sir Christopher Wren and was

home to William and Mary, Queen Anne, King George I, King

George II, Queen Victoria, and Princess Diana. The birthplace of

Queen Victoria, Kensington Palace continues as a private royal

residence, but the State Apartments and Royal Dress Collection

are open to the public and fascinating.

Visit the unique gardens and the Orangery for lunch or

tea in this beautiful setting.

Following your Palace visit, return to Broad Walk and

continue right in the direction of Kensington Road, exiting Hyde Park at the Palace Gate or the Queen's Gate. You are close to Royal Albert Hall, a world-class music and theater venue. Tours are available, but, even better,

purchase tickets for a performance. The Hall is part of an academic center that includes the Royal College of Music and Imperial College. There is also a Museum of Instruments. Follow Prince

Consort Road to Exhibition Road and turn right to

Museum Mile. On the right are the Science Museum

and the Natural History Museum, and on the left is

the Victoria and Albert Museum. All three are up-to-date, exciting environments

for visitors of all ages. The Science Museum is a destination

all its own,   and you could spend hours there. The gift

shop is full of educational and fun toys, books, and

games. At The Natural History Museum you can

explore dinosaurs, bugs,

volcanoes and earthquakes,

as well as gems and rocks.

More hours of fun! Be sure

to enter through the Cromwell Road entrance and its magnificent grand arch. Enter the Victoria and Albert Museum on Cromwell Road as well. Specializing in the decorative arts from the past

to the present, it has endless corridors and galleries including a

Frank Lloyd Wright gallery of Indian Art. Recently, showcased the costumes

and Nehru Gallery a special exhibition of the famous female

rock group from the '60s, the

Supremes. Be sure to visit the gift

shop for unusual jewelry and gifts and

do not miss the spectacular Chihuly

chandelier in the entrance gallery.

These museums charge admission, and there

is much to see, so

you may need an

extra day for museum *PowerHiking*.

Each museum has a café, but there are

some fun pubs on Brompton Road, such

as The Bunch of Grapes. The food and atmosphere are typically British, and it is quick and inexpensive.

Continue on Brompton Road into

Knightsbridge and Harrods, the

iconic British department store.

It houses seven floors of diverse

items such as gourmet foods,

chocolates, luxury

jewelry, shoes, clothing,

and even pets! Wander

around and be sure to visit the world-famous food

vaults downstairs. There are cafes, bakeries, prepared

entrées, and even tea at the famous French Ladurée.

Outside Harrods you will find lots more shopping, including Burberry,

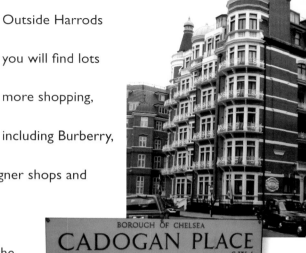

Harvey Nichols, and many other designer shops and delightful cafés.

After shopping, we *PowerHike* into the

stately neighborhood of Belgravia, location of many consulates and embassies. We are on our way to dinner at the famous Grenadier. The Grenadier is a pub located in Wilton Mews. It was the mess hall of the Duke of Wellington's Grenadier Guards and it is filled with

military memorabilia and, reputedly, the ghost of an officer accused of cheating at cards. Reservations are a must for the small restaurant, but bar food is also available. Follow Knightsbridge almost to

the Wellington Arch, turning around the corner to the right towards Grosvenor Place. Follow Grosvenor Crescent to the right and, at Belgrave Square, turn right on Wilton Crescent. Look for Wilton Mews on the right, a little dead-end alley with the famous Grenadier Pub. It is a lovely

neighborhood and the pub definitely worth the

WILTON CRESCENT SW1
CITY OF WESTMINSTER

effort to find. Enjoy a perfect ending to your

PowerHike!

TIME All day   **DISTANCE** Approximately **6** miles

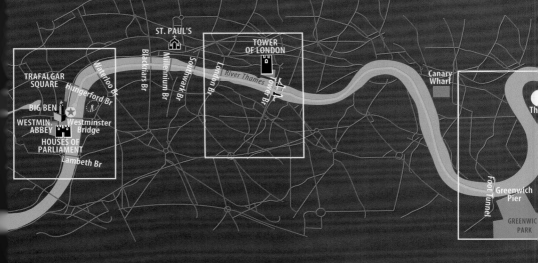
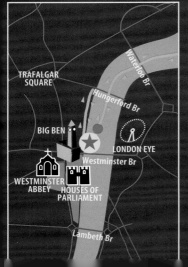

The river, infamous setting for pirates, beheadings, imprisonment, torture, and the spoils of an empire, is now filled with new life and purpose. From old London to new London, this *PowerHike* takes us on a journey through history and into the present. We start on the Victoria Embankment next to the

Westminster Bridge under the watchful eye of Big Ben. Londoners enjoy strolling Victoria Embankment taking in the sights of the river. Join them spending a few minutes strolling and admiring the architecture of the grand old buildings. As you approach the Hungerford Bridge, the beautiful Embankment Gardens are on the left. Chairs are available to rent—a wonderful location to relax and watch the activity on the river and observe the London Eye. Return

back along to the Purchase a

The Embankment water taxi terminal. ticket to Greenwich

and sit back and embark on the River Thames.

On the cruise are many of London's famous historical sites and majestic old

buildings. Passing under the Waterloo, Hungerford and Blackfriars Bridges

approaching St. Paul's Cathedral, the new skyline of the city appears. Notice

the modern buildings rising next to older buildings, including the rocket-like

building the Londoners call the Gherkin. The Millennium Bridge is a modern contrast to the bridges just passed under. Further along the

river on the right is the HMS Belfast, a cruiser that was part

of the World War II Normandy Invasion.

Tours are available. Just beyond, on the

right, is the unique City Hall, a round, black

glass modern wonder. Across the river is

the Tower

of London,

scene to

much history,

and a site to visit on the return cruise. The

famous Tower Bridge is ahead and, sailing under

it, notice the surroundings begin to change. On the left sandwiched in between apartment buildings is the Captain Kidd pub. Captain Kidd was hanged at this

pub and a visit is a step history of the river. There and modern apartment back from both banks of the Docklands, this area but is also the newest chic

into the pirate are numerous new buildings stretching the river. Known as not only is attractive, area to live. Hot

restaurants and modern hotels share

space with traditional pubs in Canary Wharf. This section of London was once

alive with warehouses full of fruit shipped from the Canary Islands. Today there

are high rise office buildings and a hotel complex.

At the Greenwich Pier disembark and follow the Embankment left to the Old

Royal Naval College. Just beyond the college on the river are two historic

pubs frequented by fishermen for centuries, a good spot for refreshment.

Return on the Embankment to the pier and King William Walk, following it to

St. Mary's Gate, and enter Greenwich Park. The park is lovely and you can visit

the National Maritime Museum, the Old Royal Observatory (through which

the Greenwich  Meridian runs),

the Planetarium, or the Queen's

House, designed by Inigo Jones.

Leaving the park, go left to Croom's

Hill and the antique market.

Greenwich is well known for antiques and the shops are a delight to peruse.

Return to the pier and step aboard the historic Cutty Sark, fastest clipper of her

time. The Greenwich Footway Tunnel leads under the water to the Isle of Dogs

across the river. Both ends of the Footway Tunnel are accessed by large round

domes. The Millennium Dome,

built to celebrate the millennium,

is the scene of many concerts and festivities. Surrounded by lakes, parks, and the

river, the Dome is popular for picnics and fun.

Return to the boat and  disembark at the Tower

Bridge Wharf. Wander to the right on St. Katharine's

Way to explore St. Katharine's Docks,

significant trade site of the 1800s. Now there are

shops, restaurants,

apartments, a yacht harbor and the Dickens Inn, a local hot spot. A little beyond

this dock area is the Prospect of Whitby. In existence since 1543 and a hangout

for smugglers, this historical pub nestles between old docks and warehouses

converted into modern apartments, and the river. A visit is an

adventure into the river's history.

Retrace your steps on St. Katharine's

Way to the Tower Bridge. Cross the

river on this famous bridge and descend

on the other

Embankment

to visit the

unique City

Hall and Hays

Galleria. Walk back

over the bridge

and follow the

cobbled Embankment path past cannon still used for royal

salutes and the infamous Traitor's Gate, to purchase your

ticket for the Tower of London. Enter through the main gate

guarded by one of the many handsomely uniformed Yeoman

HAY'S
galleria
→
RIVERSIDE
SHOPPING
&
EATING

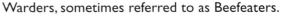

Warders, sometimes referred to as Beefeaters.
There is much to be visited inside the Tower
so be sure to allow plenty of
time. The Yeoman Warders lead
tours laced with fascinating tales
of history, intrigue, and treason.
Your visit should include Bloody
Tower, White Tower, Chapel Royal
of St. Peter ad Vincula, Royal

Fusiliers Museum (housing an astounding
collection of armor and weapons
dating from Henry VIII), Queen's House,

Traitor's Gate, and the Tower Green (location of the Tower's many beheadings, including Ann Boleyn's). Watch for one of the many ravens that make their nests at the Tower. There is even a Yeoman Raven Master to care for and feed the birds. Legend has it that the kingdom would fall if the birds ever left the Tower, so they are treated with extreme care. Perhaps the most famous part of the Tower is the Jewel House, and the Crown Jewels of

Great Britain. A mesmerizing and extremely well-displayed exhibit, you will see crowns,

On this site stood a scaffold on which were executed:

Queen Anne Boleyn Second wife of Henry VIII	19 May 1536
Margaret, Countess of Salisbury Last Plantagenet princess	27 May 1541
Queen Katherine Howard Fifth wife of Henry VIII	13 Feb 1542
Jane Viscountess Rochford Wife of Anne Boleyn's brother	13 Feb 1542
Lady Jane Grey Uncrowned Queen of 9 days	12 Feb 1554
Robert Devereaux Earl of Essex	25 Feb 1601
Lord Hastings Was also beheaded near the spot in 1483	

robes, and ornaments dating from the 1600s, worn by the English monarchy for coronations and other formal occasions. It is splendid and well worth the time. If your visit to the Tower is in the evening, be sure to watch the Ceremony of the Keys. Dating back centuries, the ceremony closes the main gate and the keys are stored at Queen's House till the morning. Your stay at the Tower would not be complete without stopping at one of the various shops for enticing souvenir replicas, historical books and DVDs.

On leaving the Tower, you may re-board the riverboat back to Westminster Bridge. It is possible to walk back along Victoria Embankment, if you prefer. Either way, take the time to marvel at the many historical wonders of London's Docklands explored on this *PowerHike*.

CHAPTER FOUR

CHELSEA GARDEN SHOW

TIME   **5** plus hours

DISTANCE   **3** plus miles
Chelsea Flower Show
2 miles   Chelsea Embankment

Garden enthusiasts from around the world make the pilgrimage to the Chelsea Flower Show each May. It is an annual rite of spring for Londoners. Even the Queen attends on Opening Day, and there are elegant festivities for dignitaries and members of the Royal Horticultural

Society. Famous landscape and garden designers compete for top recognition,

and there is always a theme (2008 was GREEN!). It is truly a visual splendor like no other and a unique and special event.

We start this *PowerHike* at The Royal

Hospital Chelsea on Royal Hospital Road just below Lower Sloane Street and Pimlico Road. The Hospital has a distinctive gift shop and museum, and you may see smartly uniformed veterans around, but visit this historic site on the Chelsea neighborhood *PowerHike*, and save your energy for the flowers.

Entering the Chelsea Flower Show is overwhelming and it is almost impossible to decide where to start. Wander Royal Hospital Way, Main Avenue, and Eastern Avenue, and you will see booths with everything from garden paintings, to gloves,

garden boots, garden tools,

garden pots, clothing,

books, seeds, posters,

souvenirs — even John

Deere tractors! To one

side are the picnic and

restaurant areas, filled

with scrumptious goodies to eat and

continuous live entertainment. On the

other side are the pavilions of fabulously

designed gardens. As you make your

way towards The Great Pavilion, there

are more small pavilions of statuary,

fencing, gates, fountains, and garden

Floral Design

furniture. There is every imaginable item one could want or use for a garden. Gather brochures to marvel at once you are back home. Entering The Grand Pavilion is an astounding visual and fragrant delight. The

enormous space is completely filled with flowers of every imaginable

bloom, and the colors and arrangements are truly spectacular. No flower is missing, and you can certainly find your favorite or a new one that you simply must

have in your garden. Be sure to collect the available catalogues and order forms
to dream over later. Allow the better part of the day to enjoy and appreciate
this gardener's fantasy.

When you can tear yourself away from the incredible beauty of the floral
displays, exit through the Chelsea Embankment Gate and turn left at the

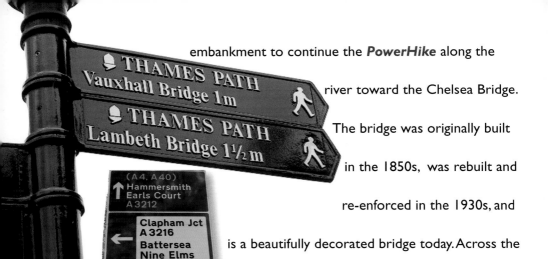

embankment to continue the *PowerHike* along the

river toward the Chelsea Bridge.

The bridge was originally built

in the 1850s, was rebuilt and

re-enforced in the 1930s, and

is a beautifully decorated bridge today. Across the

River Thames and the Chelsea Bridge

is Battersea Park. With its beach, lake,

flowers and children's zoo, Battersea

Park is an enjoyable outing.

We continue along the Chelsea

Embankment which becomes

Grosvenor Road following the river, and wander through Pimlico Gardens. Crossing

the Vauxhall Bridge, you will see the Tate Britain. Full

of fabulous exhibits, the Tate Britain is definitely worth visiting but, perhaps,

on a day saved for museums. Beyond the Tate are Lambeth Bridge and Victoria

Tower Gardens. Beautiful and tranquil, the gardens permit lovely views of the Houses of Parliament, Westminster Hall, and Big Ben, sitting serenely on the banks of the River Thames with the London Eye in the background. In another *PowerHike* you will cross the Thames to the Embankment, but for now, as a

fitting British

ending to this

PowerHike, visit

the Red Lion Pub

on Bridge Street and reflect on this glorious

and most beautiful day.

Tickets for the Chelsea Flower Show must be purchased in advance, as the entire event sells out. It takes place in May and lasts for a week. Tickets may be purchased on the internet.

TIME **3** hours   **DISTANCE** **3** miles

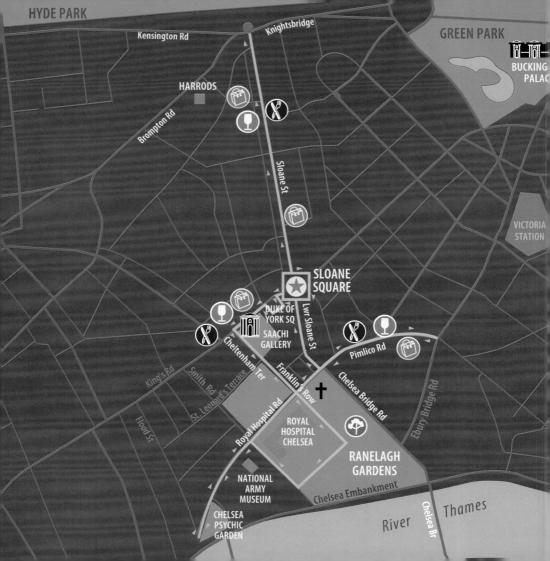

Chelsea is a chic neighborhood tucked behind Harrods department store in Knightsbridge, bordered by upscale Sloane Street, the River Thames, and King's Road. It began as a well-to-do suburb of London in the 17th century, when King's Road was a private road for Charles II to go from Buckingham Palace to Hampton Court. Only those in possession of a copper pass with the words "The King's Private Road" were allowed to use King's Road, and it remained private until the 1830s. It was quiet, filled

with trees, and a safe distance away from the grime of London. Even though London grew up around King's Road, Chelsea is still a testament to a bygone time, with stately brick buildings, grand homes, and lovely cottages, set off by well-tended squares and gardens. In the 19th century, Chelsea was inhabited by writers and artists, and through the years it has been home to painters and

authors. J.M.W. Turner, James McNeill

Whistler, John Singer Sargent, Henry

James, Bram Stoker, Thomas Wolfe, and

Mark Twain all called Chelsea home.

Today these very expensive homes

still attract celebrities, such as members of the Rolling Stones, and those who

appreciate the architecture, history, and village atmosphere between the Thames

and Hyde Park.

We start our *PowerHike* in Chelsea at Sloane

Square. Known for extraordinary shopping, the

elegant Peter Jones department store anchors

one corner, designers Montblanc and Jo Malone can be found on another, and the famous Royal Court Theatre dominates another. Some of London's best theater is presented here, an opportunity for your evening entertainment following shopping. Circle the Square, and as you start down King's Road, go left into the Duke of York Square. Filled with shops and cafés,

it is a bustling London scene. Return to King's

Road, turning left to wander one of London's finest shopping

streets. There are some not-to-be-missed shops along the way

as well as some terrific pubs and cafes. You might like Ad Hoc, a whimsical collection of style and costume pieces, or Steinberg & Tolkien features vintage clothing. Lush is a unique natural soap and cosmetics boutique, wonderful to drift through and inhale!

Smythson's is a proper English stationery store, perfect for small gifts. For the more established designer clothing, we will return to Sloane Street at the end of the *PowerHike*.

As you approach Cheltenham Terrace, turn left into the building that was Headquarters of the Duke of York, an imposing building now transformed into the Saachi Gallery, a contemporary art museum that opened in October 2008.

It hosts exciting exhibitions of contemporary art from around the world. It is open every day, and entrance is free. Continue toward the Thames on Franklin's Row to Royal Hospital Road, turning left to the Main Gate

of the Royal Hospital. You will see the Old Burial Ground just outside the gate. It is not open to the public, but you can look inside from the street.

Ten thousand soldiers are thought to be buried there. The Royal Hospital was founded by Charles II in 1682 for sick and aging war veterans, and it was built by Christopher Wren. There are still about 400 veterans who are cared for. The veterans have distinctive red and blue uniforms with tricorn hats worn on military holidays. Military buffs will love the National Army Museum. Just adjacent are Ranelagh Gardens, a large, woodsy park that extends to the River Thames. The hospital grounds and Ranelagh Gardens are the site of the Chelsea Flower Show one week each May. It attracts thousands of garden lovers from

around the world. We visit the Chelsea Flower Show on another *PowerHike*.

As you exit, continue a short distance to the left down Royal Hospital Road. You

will see the Chelsea Physic Garden, which was created in 1673 as a garden for medicinal plants. It is open from April through October, on Wednesday and Sunday, 10 a.m. to 6 p.m.

Retrace your steps on Royal Hospital Road back past the Old Burial Ground and Ranelagh Gardens, and continue straight ahead as Royal Hospital Road becomes Pimlico Road. This street is famous for antique stores and other design-oriented

businesses. In addition, there is Daylesford Organic,

a delightful café that features only organic and

sustainably farmed food. You can purchase a picnic

to take with you or eat inside or outside under the

awning at the café. A little further down Pimlico

Road is Daylesford Organic The Garden and across the street is Daylesford

Organic The Butcher. Food for Daylesford Organic comes from their farm in the

Cotswolds, and there are other Daylesford

Organic cafés around London. Circle

the small square and pass Saint Barbaras

Church of England. Just down the street

from the church is a typical Chelsea residential

neighborhood.   Return on Pimlico Road to Lower

Sloane Street and turn right, continuing on past

Sloane Square on Sloane Street. Here you will find

world famous designer shops, and it is time for

some shopping. The *PowerHike*

through Chelsea ends as Sloane

Street meets Brompton Road.

CHAPTER SIX

HAMPTON COURT

TIME   All Day   **DISTANCE**   **5** plus miles

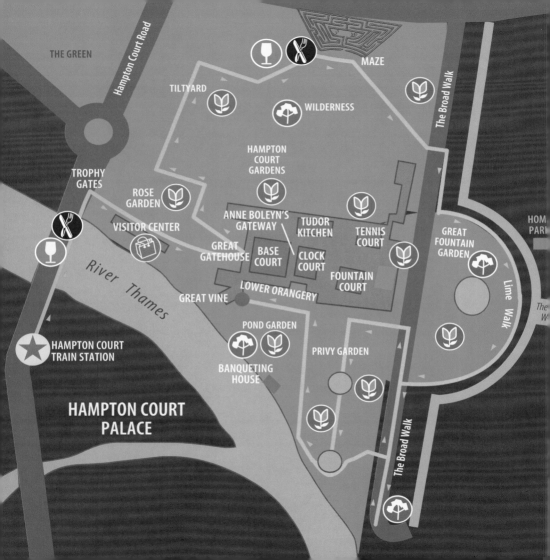

This *PowerHike* is a walk into the splendid, glorious history of England and the beauty of English gardens. We start at the famous London Waterloo Station, which can be reached by a short walk over Waterloo Bridge, by underground, or by taxi.

Purchase a round-trip ticket to Hampton Court Station and relax for a short, 40 minute ride to the English countryside. Hampton Court Palace can also be reached by

Westminster along

river launch from

the River Thames.

Located on the banks of the River Thames, Hampton

Court Palace is in a magnificent setting. As you exit

the train station, cross over the bridge to the right

and notice the charming

restaurants across the

street, Blubeckers, and Hampton's, which overlook

the river and has an outdoor patio right on the

river—a perfect spot to relax and watch

the boats go by.

Pass through the Palace gates and enter

the vast pathway leading to Hampton Court. On the left is the visitor center, where you can purchase your ticket and also visit the gift store.

A special aspect of the Palace is the appearance of various historical characters throughout the day. Be sure to check the daily program for appearances and for the time of the garden tour.

The Palace was originally a country estate, and it was Cardinal Woolsey who

began the estate's transformation. Henry VIII created the royal Palace you see today, and he lived here with each of his many wives. His contribution is the Tudor part of the palace. William and Mary attempted to change the Tudor to baroque but never finished, and the result is a palace unique in its architectural differences. Cross the bridge over the filled-in moat and pass through the Great Gatehouse into the Base Court. Through the courtyard are Anne Boleyn's Gateway and the Clock Court. Signs will

direct you up the Queen's Staircase

to the Queen's Apartments, the King's

Apartments, the Royal Chapel, and

the Woolsey Rooms—all truly sumptuous. Do visit the Tudor Kitchens for an

informative insight into the process of

providing food for the Palace. There is a

miniature of the grounds in this location,

and you might even see a period

cooking demonstration.

With over 60 acres of beautiful gardens and fountains to choose from, wander

first to the

extraordinary walled rose garden and you are in

for a visual treat. Continue on to the Tiltyard, used

by Henry VIII for jousting

tournaments, and then on

to the world famous Hampton Court Maze. Continue

through the Wilderness and 20th Century Garden,

following The Broad

Walk to The Lime Walk

and The Great Fountain

Garden, with its uniquely

shaped yew trees. Enjoy the ducks and swans and

the Jubilee Fountain in The Long Water, framed by the

beautiful lime trees. Continue

along The Broad Walk

through the yew trees to

the River Thames and back

towards the Palace. The entire length of The Broad Walk along the Palace is planted each season with a vast array of colorful flowers. The Home Park, used by Henry VIII in the 16th century for hunting and today home to deer, a golf course and summer carriage rides, is the location of the Hampton Court Flower Show each July—a truly magnificent site and event.

Before visiting The Privy Garden, be sure

to see The Royal Tennis Court. First used

by Henry VIII, the court is still in use for

tennis matches. The Privy Garden was the

King's private garden. Wander through it to

the magnificent

fence and gates

that overlook

the River

Thames. Walk

back through the arbor and left to The Knot Garden and The Ponds Garden (a sunken flower

garden). Beyond is The Great Vine, first planted in 1768 and still producing a yearly crop of grapes. The garden next to its building is never planted so as not to disturb the roots of The Great Vine. Visit the Lower Orangery Garden as you walk

back to Clock Court and down the long

pathway to exit the Palace. If you have not

already enjoyed The Tiltyard Café in Hampton Court, now is the perfect time to

visit Hampton's by the river, to reflect on the magnificent gardens and palace of

Henry VIII and this most glorious **PowerHike**.

TIME **4 to 7** hours   **DISTANCE** **4** miles

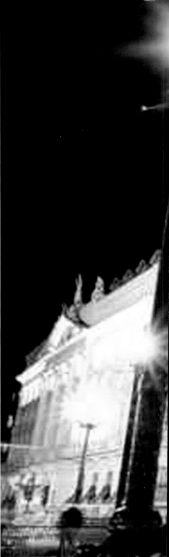

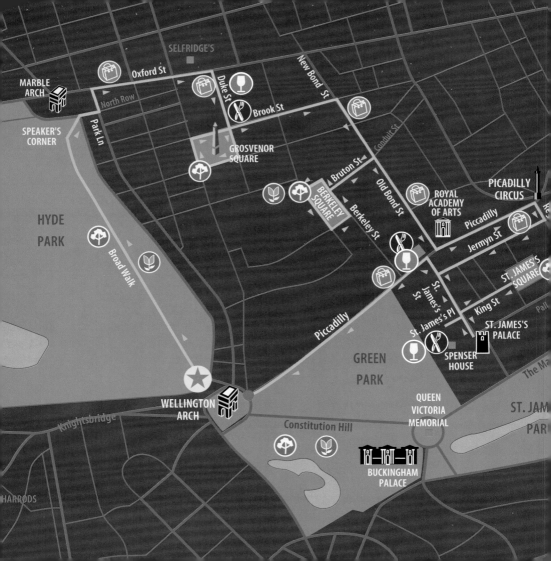

This exhilarating *PowerHike* takes you through the

finest that London has to offer: parks, squares, history,

architecture, and world-class shopping. We start at the south

east corner of

Hyde Park across

from the Wellington

Arch at the

Queen's Gate, and

walk north along

the Broad Walk,

paralleling Park Lane, in the direction of the Marble Arch. We are walking on the

western edge of the exclusive Mayfair neighborhood, which we will visit later in the walk. Notice the huge specimen trees and the

vast stretches of lawn as you walk through this serene

setting. Approaching the Marble Arch, you will see

the famous Speaker's Corner, where anyone can stand

on a soapbox and expound on any subject, except

blasphemy, obscenity, or incitement to riot. In the

1700s, before the Marble Arch was erected, Speaker's

Corner was a place of public hangings. Each prisoner

was allowed a final speech, and although there are no more hangings, the public

speaking continues, and the best sometimes is the heckling from the audience. It

is quite a fascinating and colorful spot.

At the exit of Hyde Park, straddling Park Lane and the busy thoroughfares of Bayswater Road and Oxford Street, is the magnificent Marble Arch. Built

by architect John Nash and modeled after

the Constantine Arch in Rome, the Marble

Arch was intended to be the front gate of

Buckingham Palace. However, it proved to be

too narrow for the state carriage and was

moved in 1851 to its present location. There

are actually three rooms in the arch, one across the

top and two on the sides.

Turn right onto Oxford Street, a bustling shopping

artery for Londoners. To the left is Marylebone and

Regents Park, but stay on Oxford Street, full of traffic,

buses, people, and lively activity in

every direction. One of the longest

commercial streets in the world and

location of department stores such

as Marks & Spencer and Selfridges,

with its very large perfume and cosmetics section,

Oxford Street is crammed with shoppers. The

stores are great fun and worth venturing into,

but the best of London shopping is yet to come.

Continue straight on Oxford Street to Duke Street, turning right four blocks to

Grosvenor Square, home to the American Embassy and the Canadian Embassy.

Walk through this beautiful square and relish the memorials from Eisenhower and World War II to the Roosevelt Monument.

Continue up Brook Street to New Bond Street.

High fashion begins on New Bond, with upscale

 stores such as Chanel, Donna

Karan, Gucci, Hermes, Lalique,

and Versace, and exciting jewelry

stores such as Tiffany and Cartier. Sotheby's, the

famous auction house, is on this street as well, and even has a popular tea room

 for lunch, the place to be seen! Turn

right on Bruton Lane and continue

one block to Berkeley Square

(pronounced "Barkley"). Winston

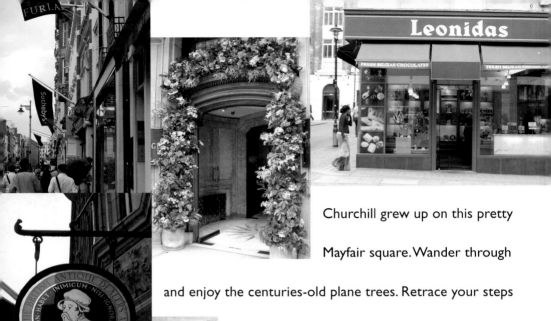

Churchill grew up on this pretty Mayfair square. Wander through and enjoy the centuries-old plane trees. Retrace your steps back toward New Bond Street, turning right and continuing as it becomes Old Bond Street at the Royal Arcade. Known for expensive jewelry, Old Bond Street is a special London treat. At the corner of Piccadilly is the famous Burlington Arcade, a

passageway

of antiques

and luxury

shops. Just

adjacent to the Burlington Arcade entrance

on Piccadilly is the Royal Academy of Arts,

housed in a beautiful 18th century mansion, Burlington House.

Across Piccadilly is the world-famous luxury food and department

store, Fortnum & Mason.

Browse the enticing

gourmet food aisles as

this is a perfect spot

to purchase treasures

to take home. The

little Fortnum & Mason

shopping bags are

status symbols in themselves! Try the traditional tearoom that serves light as well as typically English fare all day. For a fancy, old-fashioned English tea, complete with finger sandwiches, scones, clotted cream, and pastries, one of the best is found at Brown's Hotel on Albemarle Street, just off of Piccadilly past Old Bond Street. Another wonderful spot for full English tea is

the Ritz Hotel, just up Piccadilly, but reservations and proper dress are required

at both hotels. Across the street is The Wolsey, equally famous but a little more casual, where the hot chocolate is the best in London and the traditional tea service is exemplary. Breakfast, too, is a special occasion!

Exit Fortnum & Mason on Piccadilly and continue to the right until you reach

Piccadilly Circus. This is London's Times Square. Five streets come together in

this location with eye-popping traffic, electronic

signs, and hundreds of people milling about.

The fountain and winged nude statue in the

center were installed in 1893 to honor Lord

Shaftsbury, a famous politician and philanthropist.

Although the statue is thought to be Eros, the

Greek god of love, it was actually intended to

be his twin brother, Anteros. Now, popularly known as the entrance to the

theater district, Piccadilly Circus is a meeting place for those heading out for an evening's entertainment in the West End and

Soho. The name Piccadilly derives from a famous

dressmaker who lived there in the 1600s and

designed a frilled collar called a piccadil.

There are many exciting possibilities for continuing this

PowerHike from here, to Covent Garden, Soho, or Fleet

Street. We visit them all in other walks, so turn right on Regent Street and stroll

one block to Jermyn Street, filled with tailors, shoemakers, shirt makers, and hat

makers, many in this location since the 1800s.

Jermyn Street is where the well-dressed English

gentleman shops and you can find a handsome

tie or beautifully tailored shirts and suits, or

have an elegant pair of shoes made. Many stores will

have the royal coat of arms above the door, signifying

that they are merchants to the royal family. There are a

few specialty shops for ladies as well, including Fortis, a

fragrance shop filled with wonderfully scented soaps and

lotions. One stylish passageway is lined with exceptional

shops offering English china, crystal, toy soldiers

and other collectibles.

Follow Jermyn Street to St. James's Street and

turn left toward St. James's Palace. As you walk

down St. James's Street, you will pass Lock & Co.

Hatters, makers of hats to royalty since 1759. At

King Street take a quick detour to the left and visit St. James's Square. Surrounded by distinguished old buildings where many famous people, including prime ministers, have lived and several private clubs are located, the square is a beautiful oasis of magnificent big trees. Retrace your steps to St. James's Street and continue on to St. James's Palace, a small enclave

steeped in royalty. The former Queen

Mother resided here, Prince Charles has a residence here, and mail from Buckingham Palace is hand delivered back and forth daily. Also housed in the imposing classic buildings are the Architecture Foundation and Christie's. Return up

the other side of St. James's Street toward Piccadilly. At St. James's Place turn left to venture into a handsome neighborhood on the edge of Green Park. Turn left at the first small alley to Dukes Hotel, a charming, upscale boutique hotel with a superb dining room for a special dinner. As you continue on St. James's Place, there are many stately mansions on the left which back up to Green Park. One of the mansions is Spencer House, belonging to the family of

Princess Diana. The Stafford Hotel, another lovely and typically English boutique hotel, is on the right. Enjoy the American Bar where the walls are covered with American memorabilia and you can order a light meal, served on a lap tray if you wish. Retrace your steps to St. James's Street and be sure not to miss the two stores at the corner catering to the country set, where everything needed for riding and shooting can be found. One store is for gentlemen, and one for ladies. Wander through for a glimpse into

country life of the upper class in England.

Leaving the stores, turn left and continue

to Piccadilly, where you will find yourself at

the famous Ritz Hotel on Green Park. The

doormen frown on casual visitors, but if

you are properly dressed you can go in for

a look around. Back on Piccadilly, turn left

toward Green

Park and walk past the many elegant buildings and

hotels. Before you know it you will be back at the

Wellington Arch having enjoyed a *PowerHike* filled

with the best that London has to offer.

CITY OF
WESTMINSTER

CHAPTER EIGHT

THE QUEEN'S WALK

WESTMINSTER BRIDGE

LONDON EYE

TATE MODERN

MILLENNIUM BRIDGE

SAINT PAUL'S CATHEDRAL

FLEET STREET

THE STRAND

SOMERSET HOUSE

TIME All Day

DISTANCE **8** to **10** miles

depending on choice of direction

PowerHike the Queen's Walk along the South Embankment of the River Thames. Dubbed the Jubilee Walk in honor of the Jubilee (50 year) anniversary of the reign of Queen Elizabeth II, this *PowerHike* is one rich experience after another

along the banks of the Thames, including heart-stopping thrills, mind-expanding art, stunning architecture, exciting theatre, shopping, restaurants, history, and beloved English culture. Astonishingly beautiful flowerbeds, delightful dolphin lampposts, and

the magnificent London Eye make this an

exceptional walk.

We start this *PowerHike* at Westminster

Abbey and Big Ben, crossing over the

Westminster Bridge. As you cross the bridge, enjoy the

beauty of the river in both directions and the spectacular

view back at

Westminster Abbey

and Big Ben. To the

left is the South Bank Lion at the entrance

to the beautiful tree-lined walkway, and

the glorious London Eye. Built in honor of the millennium, this amazing Ferris

wheel has become a landmark of the London skyline. Buy a ticket and step into

the enormous cars for a slow but thrilling ride above London. The views are

spectacular in all directions and not to be missed. On the right, just before the

London Eye, is County Hall, which houses an aquarium that descends stories

below the Thames, an electronic
arcade, and the Dali Universe. A
little beyond is Jubilee Gardens,
a beautiful spot to relax and

observe the river and the Eye. Stop to watch the mimes and street performers,

and, as you stroll along, notice the various cafes, shops, pubs, and restaurants,

vibrant with Londoners and tourists. The bridges that span the river are all

unique and

worthy of

notice. Beyond

the Hungerford Bridge are the Royal Festival

Hall, Queen Elizabeth Hall, a smaller concert venue, the National Film Theatre,

and IMAX Cinema. Beyond Waterloo Bridge is the National Theatre. At lively

Gabriel's Wharf there are many shops and outdoor tables where you can enjoy

refreshment. The gardens nearby are a perfect

spot in which to linger and enjoy the river. Inside

the OXO Tower are several good restaurants

with terrific river views.

Passing Blackfriar's Bridge you will see the

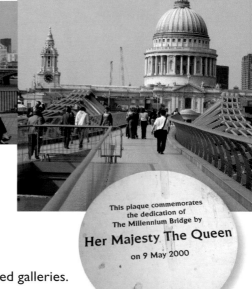

Tate Modern. Built inside an abandoned

power plant, the museum interior is

starkly unique, and the modern art is

enhanced by the expansive and well-lighted galleries.

This plaque commemorates
the dedication of
The Millennium Bridge by
Her Majesty The Queen
on 9 May 2000

The restaurant on the

top floor has incredible views of the city, the river,

and St. Paul's Cathedral, with its dome dominating

the view, a perfect setting for tea. Next to the Tate

Modern is the Globe Theatre, an exact replica of Shakespeare's original Globe Theatre. What fun to plan time to see a performance or take a tour!

When exiting the Tate and the Globe Theatre, cross the Millennium Bridge.

Opened in 2000, the footbridge was quite shaky and unstable at first but has since been stabilized. Once back on the other side of the Thames, you can *PowerHike* to the left on The Embankment, enjoying a stroll along the other side of the river, back to Westminster Abbey and the end of an exciting *PowerHike*.

If you want to continue, walk straight ahead to St. Paul's Cathedral. Designed by Christopher

Wren in the late 1600s and completed in 1708, the church is an inspiring sight, with its grand dome and double spires. The inside is magnificent, and you might even hear a choral performance. There is the Whispering Gallery, a climb to the dome for amazing views, the crypt,

and a café. St. Paul's Cathedral is a quieting respite in the midst of the bustling

city. As you leave St. Paul's, follow Ludgate Hill which becomes Fleet Street. The Royal Courts of Justice are on the right and if

you are lucky, you will see a barrister in traditional

robe and wig. Fleet Street is now a noisy, busy, crowded street, but was once the

heart of the English publishing industry.

Most publishers have moved to the

Docklands (another *PowerHike*), but the

historic old buildings remain. If you prefer

to avoid the crowds and bustle, you can

return to The Embankment from St. Paul's. Fleet Street connects to The Strand and at Somerset House you can escape to the serenity of its unusual fountain and relative quiet of The Embankment as you return to our starting point at Westminster Abbey. You can also continue on The Strand to Whitehall, turning left for your return to Westminster Abbey, a perfect location to find a pub in which to relax and reflect on the extraordinary places you have visited in this *PowerHike*.

CHAPTER NINE

TRAFALGAR SQUARE AND COVENT GARDEN

TIME **5** to **6** hours   **DISTANCE** **6** miles

TRAFALGAR SQUARE WC2
CITY OF WESTMINSTER

Trafalgar Square is the heart of London, where once upon a time royalty played, history and art merged, and the food merchants of London sold their produce under a huge glass roof. Today it is a central part of the city and the site of great bustle, where people gather on holidays, for rallies, and just to see and be seen. Visitors to London go to Trafalgar Square to see the famous column and statue honoring Admiral

Nelson for his greatest victory over the French and Spanish in the Battle of Trafalgar. Art lovers visit the National Gallery to view some of the most famous paintings dating from the 13th century to 1900. Those going to the theater flock

to Covent Garden for the newest plays

and musicals, pubs and restaurants.

The main thoroughfare into Trafalgar

Square is The Mall. Our *PowerHike* walks

The Mall but begins at the Wellington Arch.

Walk

through

Green Park to the Queen

Victoria Memorial and

left on The Mall, the wide,

leafy avenue connecting Buckingham Palace to

Whitehall and Westminster, used by the royals

for ceremonial occasions such as the Opening of Parliament and Trooping the

Color. Walk along this historic route admiring the grand architecture. Clarence

House, on the left, is now occupied by

Prince Charles. You will also pass the

Queen's Chapel, Marlborough House, the

Duke of York Column, and Waterloo Place.

St. James's Park is on the right and The

Mall is frequently adorned with grand flags

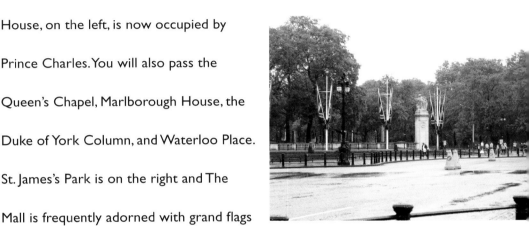

and banners. At the end of The Mall is the imposing Admiralty Arch and your

entry into Trafalgar Square. The fountain

is magnificent and there are always many

tourists, as well as locals, milling about

enjoying the scene. Beyond the square is the classic

façade and impressive staircase of the National

Gallery and the National Portrait Gallery. A world

class art museum not to be missed, the National

Gallery houses an enormous collection of paintings

displayed in elegant, well-lighted galleries. The collection is organized by school, so you can easily find your favorites. Crivelli's Garden in the Sainsbury Wing is an excellent spot for refreshment.

After your visit to the National Gallery, walk around to the left on Trafalgar Square and you will see the Church of St. Martin-in-the-Fields on the northeastern corner. Its architecture may seem familiar, as it was often copied in the United States. You can enjoy free chamber music concerts, and the famous choir performs for Sunday services.

Continue left up St. Martin's Lane to Litchfield Street and west to Ivy, one of the most fashionable restaurants in London. Dining there is an event and

reservations are a must. Return to Trafalgar Square and continue around to the southeast corner to a small granite pillar, known as London's smallest police station! One officer can barely fit inside.

Leaving Trafalgar Square, *PowerHike* up The Strand in the direction of Charing Cross Station, one of the busiest transportation sites in London. The Strand was once a main thoroughfare in the city and now joins Trafalgar Square to the City of London (the business center of London). On the right is

the famous Savoy Hotel, and, just beyond, Somerset House. Go inside Somerset

House to escape the traffic and to mosey though the incredible fountain, with

water spouting out of the ground. The fountain becomes an ice skating rink

in winter. At Wellington, turn left and enter Covent Garden. As you go along,

you can enjoy the scene of people, window

shop, and check out the pubs. The Lyceum

Theater, on the corner, was built in 1771 and is

currently owned by Andrew

Lloyd Webber. Wellington

becomes Bow Street, and you will come to The Royal Opera

House, home to the Royal Ballet and the Royal Opera. Recent

renovations brought state-of-the-art set changing to the

venue, and backstage tours are offered everyday except Sunday. On your right

on Catherine Street before you reach The Royal Opera House is the Theatre

Royal, Drury Lane, opened by royal charter in 1663. There is so much history

in this theater that taking the tour is a must. They are

available everyday, for no charge. Wander through

the squares and streets, Long Acre

the most famous, enjoying the many shops,

restaurants and outdoor musical and theatrical

performances. Floral Street is an enchanting

cobbled street that, in years past, was home to

the florists of London. Today, there are many

upscale designer shops. You will definitely want

to stop for refreshment

at one of the many

chic and crowded

establishments in this

very trendy district. The Lamb and Flag on

Floral Street, opened in 1663, was a favorite

of Charles Dickens.

The Covent Garden Market is on Southampton

Street and we pass it as we make our way

back to The Strand. The name, Covent Garden,

originates from the convent garden in Westminster Abbey, which once stood on this spot. A residential area that was a flower and vegetable market from 1860 to 1974, the market with its huge Victorian glass roof today houses a mall featuring shops, cafes, pubs, sidewalk entertainment, and crowds of people having fun. St. Paul's Church is nearby, the location of the opening scene from Pygmalion, where Professor Higgins meets Eliza Doolittle selling flowers. At The Strand,

turn right and walk through the heart of the London theater district back

toward Trafalgar Square. There will certainly be a play or musical of interest so plan to return on another evening for some wonderful entertainment and dinner in one of the many busy restaurants along the way.

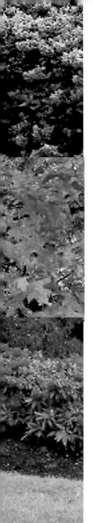

CHAPTER TEN

ROYAL BOTANIC GARDENS

KEW

PRINCESS OF WALES CONSERVATORY

PALM HOUSE

RHIZOTRON AND XSTRATA TREETOP WALKWAY

KEW PALACE

TEMPERATE HOUSE

TIME All Day

DISTANCE 2 miles from the station to the Gardens and back **5** to **6** miles in the Gardens

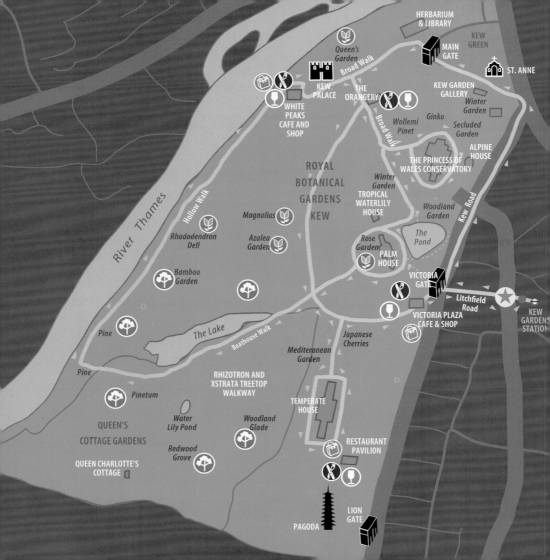

HERBARIUM & LIBRARY

MAIN GATE

KEW GREEN

ST. ANNE

Queen's Garden

Broad Walk

KEW PALACE

THE ORANGERY

KEW GARDEN GALLERY

Winter Garden

WHITE PEAKS CAFE AND SHOP

Wollemi Pinet

Ginko

Secluded Garden

Broad Walk

THE PRINCESS OF WALES CONSERVATORY

ALPINE HOUSE

ROYAL BOTANICAL GARDENS KEW

Winter Garden

TROPICAL WATERLILY HOUSE

Woodland Garden

The Pond

Kew Road

Hollow Walk

Magnolias

River Thames

Rhododendron Dell

Azalea Garden

Rose Garden

PALM HOUSE

VICTORIA GATE

Litchfield Road

KEW GARDENS STATION

Bamboo Garden

VICTORIA PLAZA CAFE & SHOP

Pine

The Lake

Boathouse Walk

Japanese Cherries

Mediteranean Garden

Pine

RHIZOTRON AND XSTRATA TREETOP WALKWAY

TEMPERATE HOUSE

Pinetum

Water Lily Pond

Woodland Glade

QUEEN'S COTTAGE GARDENS

Redwood Grove

RESTAURANT PAVILION

QUEEN CHARLOTTE'S COTTAGE

PAGODA

LION GATE

A **PowerHike** through *Kew Gardens, a World Heritage Site*, is a most beautiful, picturesque and inspiring walk. Located just 10 km. outside of London, and easily reached by public transportation, car or boat, this world-famous botanical center is in the forefront of research today on plants and their role in our lives and the environment. There are over 300 fabulous acres of gardens, specimen trees, beautiful glass conservatories, a palace,

and even a botanical art gallery. In addition, there are tempting cafes and shops, special

exhibits, and marvels for the whole family. You can *PowerHike* the entire garden,

or choose to get on and off the Kew Explorer, a train that circles the grounds

with narration by knowledgeable drivers. Even in the rain, the Gardens are

beautiful and, with the Kew Explorer, you can enjoy the Gardens and stay dry.

Kew Gardens is a *PowerHiking* adventure for every season and one definitely

not to be missed.

Kew Gardens can be reached by the District Line underground in the direction

of Richmond, getting off at Kew Gardens. You can also take a riverboat from

Westminster, Richmond or Kingston-upon-

Thames. Follow the signs and it is a short

walk through town to Kew Road and

the Main Gate on the river side of

Kew Gardens via
Kew Green 1.1m/1.8km

River Thames 1.3m/2.1km

Kew Pier for Boats
1.4m/2.3km

the Gardens. Pick up a map at the gate, and start your *PowerHike* on Broad Walk straight into the center of the Park. Be sure to note

the spectacular trees along the way as you walk. The beauty and diversity of the trees is exquisite. As you turn onto Broad Walk, you will pass The Orangery Restaurant, a delightful place for a snack in a beautiful building, on your way to the imposing Princess of

Wales Conservatory. The structure contains 10 different computer-controlled tropical habitats covering all conditions in the tropics, from desert to rainforest. The Conservatory was opened by Diana, Princess of Wales, in 1987, and commemorates Princess Augusta, who founded the Gardens in 1736. Be sure to visit the Davies Alpine House, built in 2006 specifically for alpine plants, keeping them dry and cool, and the Bonsai House just beyond the Conservatory.

Continue on Broad Walk to the Palm House, the most iconic building in the Park,

and the most important surviving Victorian glass and iron structure in the

world. It was built to house the exotic palm trees coming into Europe during

the Victorian era, thus its impressive height. It is a world-famous Grade 1 listed building, even though it has been restored twice. There is also a fascinating display of marine plants in its lower

level. Do not miss the beautiful Pond across the way, the Rose Garden behind

the Palm House, and the Waterlily House just across the road.

Now is a good time to hop on the Kew Explorer and enjoy a narrated tour of the far end of the Gardens. The trees are magnificent, all planted in groups. You

will pass the Woodland Glade, the Pinetum, the Waterlily Pond, the Bamboo

Garden, a large lake,

the Rhododendron

Dell, the Azalea

Garden, and the

Park's newest feature,

the Treetop Walk,

opened in May 2008.

You can walk along

the tops of the trees as well as below the surface to see the root structure. It is

truly a fascinating experience. As the train circles around, get off at White Peaks

Café & Shop. The Café is a perfect spot for tea, and the White Peaks Children's

Shop is worth exploring for imaginative and educational children's toys.

Kew Palace is just beyond White Peaks located on the river side of the Gardens.

It is open March through September, and the Queen's Garden in the Palace is

lovely. Built in 1631 by a London merchant, the brick palace became the family

home of King George III and Queen

Charlotte, and their many children.

On the other side of the Gardens is

Queen Charlotte's Cottage, a simple,

rustic tea and picnic house built by

the famous gardener, Capability Brown, for the royal family. Leave Kew Palace

and follow Broad Walk towards the other side of

the Park. Turn at Cherry Walk to Temperate House,

the largest glass house at Kew, now the world's

largest surviving Victorian glass structure. It houses

woody plants from subtropical and warm regions

all over the world. Continue on, passing the Pavilion

Restaurant, to the Pagoda, and circle back to the Victoria Gate. There you will find the Terrace Café and a wonderful shop with irresistible garden accessories, plants, and garden books, as well as cookbooks and other gifts.

Kew Gardens is open year-round, except Christmas Eve and Christmas Day. Each season has its own charms, such as ice skating in winter! There are so many stunning

vistas, and small places of interest such as the many follies or small ornamental structures. The four gates are famous works of art in themselves and worth exploring. The water features are spectacular, along with the many species of birds and waterfowl. Exit through Victoria Gate and wander up

the charming tree-lined street through the delightfully quaint and quiet village back to the

rail station. Who would imagine that such an incredibly beautiful spot is only a

few minutes from bustling London?

Note: At the Main Gate, be sure to ask about the daily, narrated walking tours and the weekly tree-identification tours.

CHAPTER ELEVEN

NOTTING HILL

HYDE PARK

MARBLE ARCH

ITALIAN GARDENS

PRINCESS DIANA MONUMENT

PORTOBELLO ROAD

TIME All day   **DISTANCE** 11 miles

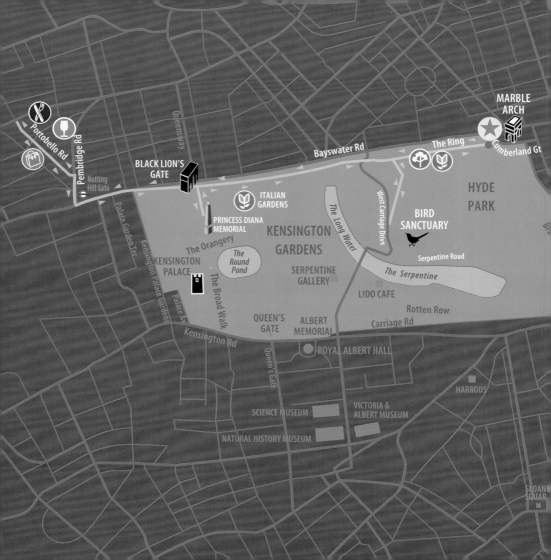

Notting Hill is a fascinating, trendy, and upscale neighborhood full of fashionable, beautiful homes. Portobello Road is its main commercial street and an enthralling experience of

shopping, pubs, and restaurants. Saturday is wildly popular, as it is market day and

throngs of shoppers descend on the street to find a bargain. Tables selling everything from antiques and silver to fruits and vegetables line both sides of Portobello Road for its entire length.

We start our *PowerHike* to Notting Hill at the Marble

Arch in Hyde Park. The arch straddles Bayswater Road

and Oxford Street

at the northeast corner of Hyde Park. Walk

into the park and onto The Ring, a wide

path on the north

side of the park that

parallels Bayswater Road. This part of the park is quite dense with trees, and

there are many paths to wander, as well as a bird sanctuary. Explore some of the

different paths   leading to Long Water,

home to flocks   of ducks and birds.

You will come to   Queen Anne's Alcove

and the Italian Gardens. At this point, follow the signs to the Princess Diana

Monument, a truly unique and inspiring part of the

park. Exit Hyde Park at the Black Lion Gate and turn

left onto Bayswater Road.

At Pembridge Road and the Notting Hill Gate, turn

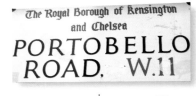

right. Two blocks down on the left is Portobello Road, a famous landmark in the Notting Hill neighborhood and the location of fruit and vegetable vendors since the 1800s. On Saturdays, it comes alive as it is market day and vendors line the street from one end to the other. It seems as if there is not a thing that cannot be found here! You will find jewelry, books, old records, paintings, clothing, maps, and antiques. There is even a shop full of swords, and silver everywhere. It is a shopper's paradise! Whatever unique or unusual piece you are looking for,

you will find it. For example, charming English

teapots and anything associated with tea making

can be found. It is a good place to find small

gifts and souvenirs. There are crowds of people

at the market, so the best way to enjoy it and

not miss that special treasure is to walk down

one side and back

up the other. Keep

walking toward the

end of the road to the fruit and vegetable vendors.

Indulge, enjoy, and be sure to step into one of the

local pubs for refreshment before returning up the

road. Beware:
There is no
shipping, so you
must carry your
treasures.
(If you succumb
to temptation

and end up with your arms full of must-haves, you can find a taxi fairly easily on

one of the side streets.)

Otherwise, return to Notting

Hill Gate and Bayswater Road.

This busy road is crowded with